PUBLISHED by PARABLES
Earthly Stories with a Heavenly Meaning

The Judgments Of God

By
Cynthia Alvarez

Earthly Stories with a Heavenly Meaning

The Judgments Of God
Cynthia Alvarez

Published By Parables
October, 2019

All Rights Reserved. No part of this book may be reproduced or utilized in any form or by any means, electronic or mechanical, including photocopying, recording, or by any information storage and retrieval system, without permission in writing from the author.

ISBN 978-1-951497-06-4
Printed in the United States of America

Readers should be aware that Internet Web sites offered as citations and/or sources for further information may have been changed or disappeared between the time this was written and the time it is read.

The Judgments Of God

By
Cynthia Alvarez

CONTENTS

Chapter One
Judgment of Sin
Page 5

Chapter Two
Judgment Seat of Christ
Page 19

Chapter Three
Judgment of the Israel
Page 35

Chapter Four
Judgment of the Nations
Page 57

Chapter Five
The Great White Throne Judgment
Page 73

PREFACE

The spiritual winds of change are being ushered into this earthly realm like never before, as we see compelling evidence and an ever unfolding reality of the closing days of this Age of Grace that we are so accustomed to in this generation. Yet, God's sovereign hand and preordained will continues to govern every age of humanity's existence on this earthly plateau. Although many people see this current age as a perpetual reality of existence, they have little to no understanding of what is next on the agenda of God's sovereignty, which happens to be the judgment of all humanity. For many people the thought of judgment is farfetched because they have not come to terms with the existence of a sovereign God who rules heaven and earth. And not only is He the Sovereign God, but He is the God of justice in all things. So, being the God of justice means that He must deal fairly and righteously in judgment concerning His creation. With these aspects of His character on the table so to speak, God has prepared five judgments that will be for the sole purpose of judging humanity. Different classifications of humanity will be associated or assigned to their respective judgments as predetermined by God. The basis and outcome of these judgments will have specific characteristics that pertain to distinct classifications of individuals who will be found in them. So, this book is written to help the readers comprehend the judgments of God and to identify which judgment they will be assigned to, according to the many factors which surround their earthly lives. Please note that this book is not to condemn anyone, but to enlighten your understanding to what is next on God's sovereign agenda. I pray that everyone who reads 'The Judgments of God' will be blessed in some way and will be hard pressed to share this material with others who need to better understand God as it relates to every judgment He has established for the evaluation of His creation, humanity.

Eternal Blessings,

Cynthia Alvarez

Cynthia Alvarez

Chapter 1
Judgment of Sin

The discussion of judgment is not always the most comfortable subject for believers because it is a subject that is least understood by many Christians. However, believers should never view judgment as something to avoid in conversation, but rather it should be a topic that is welcomed at any table of discussion among believers. Yes, addressing judgment can be quite confusing and ambiguous when those attempting to tackle it lack the essential insight to rightly divide the word of God. The five judgments that will be discussed throughout this book were based on prophecy. And if prophecy is at the center of these judgments, we must understand specific details surrounding the nature or characteristics of each judgment to help us properly identify the place they hold in the ever unfolding plan of God. We must also be cognizant of the fact that everyone who has ever been born since the foundation of the world will be judged according to the condition or status of their spirit and nature of the deeds they have performed.

"Marvel not at this: for the hour is coming, in the which all that are in the graves shall hear his voice, And shall come

forth; they that have done good, unto the resurrection of life; and they that have done evil, unto the resurrection of damnation. I can of mine own self do nothing: as I hear, I judge: and my judgment is just; because I seek not mine own will, but the will of the Father which hath sent me." (John 5:28-30)

Although everyone will be judged according to the righteous standards of God, they will not all be judged at the same time or in the same place of judgment. It must be on this wise, since throughout history God has dealt with humanity in various ways. So, it would contradict His righteous and just character to attribute one judgment to all humanity when the basis of the judgment rests upon different interactions and undertakings He has had with humanity over a 6,000 year span of time. But what we do know is all of humanity will be judged on the basis of sin and works, as scripture has revealed. And what we must learn to do is rightly divide the word of God concerning the truth of His judgments. As believers in Christ, we are duty-bound to further increase our knowledge and understanding of the things concerning His will, with judgment being an inclusive aspect of such essential matters.

"Study to shew thyself approved unto God, a workman that needeth not to be ashamed, rightly dividing the word of truth." (II Timothy 2:15)

For us to rightly divide the word of God concerning His judgments, we must revisit His first interaction with man and the conditions surrounding it. Remember that throughout history He has dealt with humanity in various ways. These various ways can be seen through numerous dispensations of time where He allotted space, so that man could be proved or tested as it related to obedience. As we journey back in time to the creation of man, we see that Adam, being the first of humanity, was created as a flawless being. Adam had no knowledge or affiliation with sin or death in this flawless state. Yet, Adam was created with a free-will, which brought the possibility of sin to the forefront. God created him with a free-will, but that free-will had to be tested. In other words, Adam's standing with God had to be officially proven or validated because he was being appointed dominion over the works of God as it pertained to the earth. Although Adam's testing involved fruit from the tree of the knowledge of good and evil, the fruit was not the object being tested. Adam's free-will was being tested or evaluated to affirm his loyalty and faithfulness to God.

"And the LORD God commanded the man, saying, of every tree of the garden thou mayest freely eat: But of the tree of the knowledge of good and evil, thou shalt not eat of it: for in the day that thou eatest thereof thou shalt surely die." (Genesis 2:16-17)

Unfortunately, Adam proved that his free-will was not completely submitted to the God of heaven and earth. So, sin entered in the heart of not only Adam, but it became an intricate and dominating aspect of the nature of all generations to come. Yes, sin breached and altered the nature of the descendants of Adam forever. And wherever sin is manifested, judgment must follow. Please understand that this was not the first encounter God had with His creation that involved sin. He had already experienced a similar scenario in the heavenly realm with Satan, who was also created with a free-will. Satan's sin of rebellion resulted in great judgment because he was forced out of the third heaven where God dwells, given a judicial sentence of 1,000 years in the bottomless pit during the Kingdom Age, and afterwards, appointed to the lake of fire for eternity. Although judgment has been established concerning Satan for sin, he has only experienced one aspect of judgment, which was expulsion from the third heaven that took place in eternity past. The other aspects of his judgment are to take place in the future, and all believers should be in great anticipation to see the fulfillment of these judgements that are appointed to Satan, seeing he is forever an adversary of the King and Kingdom.

- ## Satan's First Judgment – (Past Judgment)

Expulsion from Heaven

> "And he said unto them, I beheld Satan as lightning fall from heaven." (Luke 10:18)

- ## Satan's Second Judgment – (Future Judgment)

Bound in the Bottomless Pit for 1,000 years

> "And I saw an angel come down from heaven, having the key of the bottomless pit and a great chain in his hand. And he laid hold on the dragon, that old serpent, which is the Devil, and Satan, and bound him a thousand years, And cast him into the bottomless pit, and shut him up, and set a seal upon him, that he should deceive the nations no more, till the thousand years should be fulfilled: and after that he must be loosed a little season." (Revelation 20:1-3)

- # Satan's Final Judgment – (Future Judgment)

Eternity in the Lake of Fire

> *"And the devil that deceived them was cast into the lake of fire and brimstone, where the beast and the false prophet are, and shall be tormented day and night for ever and ever."* (Revelation 20:10)

If we are to comprehend the reason for judgment, we must start by understanding that in the Kingdom of God sin is considered a crime, felony, or transgression against God, not a fluke or accident. God goes to great lengths to ensure that His will is established and known to humanity and this can be seen through His word, His Spirit, the ministry of His Fivefold Officers, as well as the very conscience of man. To know the will of God and to blatantly reject it is to become a rebel against the King and the Kingdom of God in its entirety. Such actions are punishable by law, but not law by the standards of man. It is punishable by the laws of the Kingdom of God. Too often, man has considered this current age of Grace as the standard for the eternal Kingdom of God because the grace of God has been spread abroad to humanity in this age with the intent to bring all men into the saving grace of Jesus Christ. But as this age of Grace closed out and we are transitioned into the Kingdom Age, there will be a striking difference in the administration of laws and justice. The Kingdom Age will not be an age where men will be able to rely on grace to bail them out of sinful behavior. No, they will be dealt immediate judgment for such actions. During the Kingdom Age, the Lord Jesus Christ will rule with an iron fist or with a heavy hand of judgment. Sin will not be tolerated or swept under the rug. There will be no leniency concerning sin because sin of any nature presents itself as a threat to the Kingdom of God. Thus, it must be dealt with immediately and decisively.

"And out of his mouth goeth a sharp sword, that with it he should smite the nations: and he shall rule them with a rod of iron: and he treadeth the winepress of the fierceness and wrath of Almighty God. And he hath on his vesture and on his thigh a name written, KING OF KINGS, AND LORD OF LORDS." (Revelation 19:15-16)

Judgment cannot be thought of as something only associated with the temporal reality of this earthly realm, but it is something that proceeded forth from the eternal realm as seen in God's dealing with Satan. Yet, humanity's introduction to God's judgment took place in the Garden of Eden with Adam and Eve. God gave Adam a clear and precise charge that he was not to eat from the tree of the knowledge of good and evil. He even warned them of the consequences that would follow disobeying Him and choosing rather to partake of the fruit from that tree.

"And the LORD God took the man and put him into the garden of Eden to dress it and to keep it. And the LORD God commanded the man, saying, Of every tree of the garden thou mayest freely eat: But of the tree of the knowledge of good and evil, thou shalt not eat of it: for in the day that thou eatest thereof thou shalt surely die." (Genesis 2:15-17)

After they ate the fruit from the forbidden tree of the knowledge of good and evil, sin became the ultimate downfall of man. The moment Adam partook of the fruit, judgment went forth as God had declared that it would. Fellowship between God and Adam was immediately broken, and Adam was without power in and of himself to restore that fellowship. At this moment, he was spiritually dead and barred from spiritual access to God. Not only did Adam become separated from God, but his soul began to fall into a state of degeneration, as his character became marred and he was no longer a perfect being. Then his body became affected by the judgment of sin and it began the process of growing old, which would eventually lead to physical death. Why did they eat the fruit from the forbidden tree of the knowledge of good and evil? They ate it because Satan targeted the most powerful aspect of their mind, which is the imagination.

Through stimulating their imagination, he was able to lure them into exercising their free-will to carry out the desires of their own hearts instead of total adherence to the revealed will of God.

"Now the serpent was more subtil than any beast of the field which the LORD God had made. And he said unto the woman, Yea, hath God said, Ye shall not eat of every tree of the garden? And the woman said unto the serpent, We may eat of the fruit of the trees of the garden: But of the fruit of the tree which is in the midst of the garden, God hath said, Ye shall not eat of it, neither shall ye touch it, lest ye die. And the serpent said unto the woman, Ye shall not surely die: For God doth know that in the day ye eat thereof, then your eyes shall be opened, and ye shall be as gods, knowing good and evil. And when the woman saw that the tree was good for food, and that it was pleasant to the eyes, and a tree to be desired to make one wise, she took of the fruit thereof, and did eat, and gave also unto her husband with her; and he did eat. And the eyes of them both were opened, and they knew that they were naked; and they sewed fig leaves together, and made themselves aprons."
(Genesis 3:1-7)

Adam miserably failed the testing of his free-will during a time that is considered as the 'Dispensation of Innocence', which is a time that sin was not known by man until Eve entertained Satan's words and Adam yielded to Eve's desire in eating of the fruit. In fact, Adam and Eve didn't even know they were naked in the Garden of Eden because their minds were pure and untainted by any evil thoughts. But Satan put an end to such purity through deception, causing Adam to succumb to sin at the age of 33 years old. Yes, it is the same age that Jesus was when He died on the Christ. Jesus had to atone for the sins of humanity that originated in Adam. So, a perfect sacrifice had to be offered, seeing that before Adam had fallen from grace in the Garden of Eden, he was a perfect man of such age. Not only did a perfect sacrifice have to be offered, but it had to be put to death and its blood shed for the atonement of sin.

"And almost all things are by the law purged with blood; and without shedding of blood is no remission of sin."
(Hebrews 9:22)

Because shedding of blood was necessary to atone for sin, God foreshadowed this with Adam and Eve before He expelled them from the Garden of Eden. He took animal skins and clothed them, since their eyes were now open to good and evil. After eating from the forbidden tree, they became fully aware that they were naked. So, in clothing them with animal skins, God was showing the pattern of atonement, because a living animal had to be put to death to shed its blood and cover their sins. Yet, the shedding of the blood of an animal was only a temporary solution for sin because the blood of animals could not give them a new spirit and reconcile them back to God. Only the sacrifice of the perfect man from glory, Jesus Christ could do that.

"But Christ being come an high priest of good things to come, by a greater and more perfect tabernacle, not made with hands, that is to say, not of this building: For if the blood of bulls and of goats, and the ashes of an heifer sprinkling the unclean, sanctifieth to the purifying of the flesh: How much more shall the blood of Christ, who through the eternal Spirit offered himself without spot to God, purge your conscience from dead works to serve the living God?" (Hebrews 9: 11-14)

Once Jesus gave Himself as the ultimate sacrifice for the sins of the world on Calvary, He became Lord and Savior to all who believe in Him. We receive the forgiveness of sin and are reconciled to the Father. The judgment for sin was carried out on the cross and the transgressions of every believer were placed on Jesus to bear. It is because of this act of unmerited grace by Jesus that we are free from the penalty or punishment of sin. It is a done deal and it is a past judgment. Believers in Christ do not have to face condemnation because Christ himself bore the penalty of our sins.

"And every priest standeth daily ministering and offering oftentimes the same sacrifices, which can never take away sins: But this man, after he had offered one sacrifice for sins forever, sat down on the right hand of God; From henceforth expecting till his enemies be made his footstool. For by one offering he hath perfected forever them that are sanctified. " (Hebrews 10:11-14)

Now being in Christ, we need not look for another sacrifice because Jesus is the ultimate sacrifice. We as believers are justified through Christ because God the Father judged sin on Calvary with the death and shed blood of Jesus. Because judgment for believers extends beyond the judgment of sin, we must abide in Christ and move forward into sanctification and service in Him. God has set a time and place to judge those in Christ once again, but it has nothing to do with the judgment that took place on Calvary with Jesus being the sacrificial lamb for believers. In fact, the next judgment for believers' centers around our relationship with God as sons/daughters and our service or works that we have carried out in His name. We must give account of our position in Christ as son/daughters and endure chastisement from our Heavenly Father as we continue our journey in

Christ during this earthly life. Finally, we must be held accountable before Him for the works that we have performed on behalf of our King and His Kingdom. We must be found righteous in Him in every way. Let no man deceive you concerning your salvation and the future judgment that awaits believers. We have an appointment with the Lord God that cannot be circumvented.

- **Sons/Daughters of God**

    "For whom the Lord loveth he chasteneth, and scourgeth every son whom he receiveth. If ye endure chastening, God dealeth with you as with sons; for what son is he whom the father chasteneth not? But if ye be without chastisement, whereof all are partakers, then are ye bastards, and not sons. Furthermore we have had fathers of our flesh which corrected us, and we gave them reverence: shall we not much rather be in subjection unto the Father of spirits, and live? For they verily for a few days chastened us after their own pleasure; but he for our profit, that we might be partakers of his holiness. Now no chastening for the present seemeth to be joyous, but grievous: nevertheless afterward it yieldeth the peaceable fruit of righteousness unto them which are exercised thereby." (Hebrews 12:6-11)

- **Service/Works in Christ**

    "Every man's work shall be made manifest: for the day shall declare it, because it shall be revealed by fire; and the fire shall try every man's work of what sort it is." (I Corinthians 3:13)

Chapter 2
Judgment Seat of Christ

In Chapter One, we discussed the free-will of man and the need to test or evaluate his loyalty and obedience to God. Adam failed miserably, as he willfully disobeyed God's charge concerning the fruit from the tree of the knowledge of good and evil. Adam committed a crime or transgression against God, so he had to be judged. Yes, God had to judge his sin or his evil actions. Adam was judged immediately and sentenced to hard labor and death, which was a threefold process because Adam had a threefold nature (spirit, soul, and body). God made known to Adam beforehand that the penalty for sin is death, yet hard labor was included as an element of punishment. Why? Because God is not mocked and whatever a man sows, he will also reap, but in greater measure.

Adam's sentence of death

"And the LORD God commanded the man, saying, Of every tree of the garden thou mayest freely eat: But of the tree of the knowledge of good and evil, thou shalt not eat of it: for

in the day that thou eatest thereof thou shalt surely die." (Genesis 2:16-17)

Adam's sentence to hard labor

"And unto Adam he said, Because thou hast hearkened unto the voice of thy wife, and hast eaten of the tree, of which I commanded thee, saying, Thou shalt not eat of it: cursed is the ground for thy sake; in sorrow shalt thou eat of it all the days of thy life; Thorns also and thistles shall it bring forth to thee; and thou shalt eat the herb of the field; In the sweat of thy face shalt thou eat bread, till thou return unto the ground; for out of it wast thou taken: for dust thou art, and unto dust shalt thou return." (Genesis 3:17-19)

Chapter One also discusses God's antidote for the eternal judgment of sin that was placed on Adam and all of humanity. This antidote was Jesus Christ, who paid the price for sin on Cavalry for the redemption of humanity. Once Jesus offered Himself as the sacrifice for the sins of humanity, it was a done deal. He was the perfect and only sacrifice that could appease or satisfy the judgment of the Heavenly Father regarding the trespasses of humanity. And because Jesus was the perfect sacrifice for the atonement of sin, He is the only option that humanity has for salvation and reconciliation to the Heavenly Father. Jesus is the way, the truth, and the life that restores us to the Father. So, everyone who believes in Jesus and His finished work receives salvation and is reconciled to the Heavenly Father.

"Jesus saith unto him, I am the way, the truth, and the life: no man cometh unto the Father, but by me. If ye had known me, ye should have known my Father also: and from henceforth ye know him, and have seen him." (John 14:6-7)

After we avail ourselves of the finished work of Jesus Christ on Cavalry, our journey as believers commences. Not only were we saved from something, which is sin and death, but we are saved into something, which is life eternal in Christ. Being in Christ brings us into righteous standing with God, just as Adam was in righteous standing with God before the fall. Yet, we still possess a free-will, since salvation does not dispose of the free-will of a man. Salvation gives us the opportunity to walk upright before God and yield our free-will to His sovereign will. But through foreknowledge relating to Adam's free-will and disobedience, along with the finished work of Jesus Christ, God was able to give humanity power to walk upright before Him by the indwelling of His Spirit. The indwelling of His Spirit would fortify our own spirits, so that we could walk in the power of obedience. If our spirit is fortified, our minds become fortified and if our minds are strengthened, our free-will is able to root us in obedience to the sovereign will of God. This is something that Adam did not have. Adam was a perfect man who had fellowship with God and had no knowledge of sin when he was created. But we who are in Christ are a new creation or new creatures because we have what Adam did not have. No, we are not a refurbished model of Adam, but a new creation all together that is no longer identified with Adam or the old creation.

"Therefore, if any man be in Christ, he is a new creature: old things are passed away; behold, all things are become new. And all things are of God, who hath reconciled us to himself by Jesus Christ, and hath given to us the ministry of reconciliation." (II Corinthians 5:17-18)

So, now being a new creation in Christ, we must now live out a life in Christ that is suitable or acceptable to exist in His heavenly realm and worthy of ruling and reigning with Him in the Kingdom Age. It requires a higher standard of living and the highest grade of loyalty. The reason a higher standard of living is necessary is because in Christ, we are brought into the Kingdom of God and it is the Excellent

Kingdom where all things are divine. And the reason it requires the highest grade of loyalty is because nothing less will do. God has taken great care to ensure that treason of any nature never manifests in the eternal Kingdom of God as was seen in the rebellion of Satan many eons ago. Therefore, the Kingdom of God has a different nature or characteristics than Satan's Kingdom of Darkness. They are polar-opposites and cannot be joined together on any level and at any point. The differences can be identified in the Kings of the two kingdoms, the Spirit of the two kingdoms, the citizens of the two kingdoms, and agendas or eventualities of the two kingdoms. There is simply no common ground to which these two kingdoms can enter into agreement of any sort.

"Giving thanks unto the Father, which hath made us meet to be partakers of the inheritance of the saints in light: Who hath delivered us from the power of darkness, and hath translated us into the kingdom of his dear Son: In whom we have redemption through his blood, even the forgiveness of sins: Who is the image of the invisible God, the firstborn of every creature." (Colossians 1:13-15)

Even though sin was already judged on Calvary, it does not mean that we are free from ever being judged by God again. In fact, being in Christ means that we have been appointed to a specific time and place of judgment, which will be predicated on our walk and works as believers in Christ. And this time and place of judgment is revealed to us in the bible as the Judgment Seat of Christ. It is where our walk and works will be placed on trial or evaluated by Jesus Christ Himself. It is the time and place that each believer will be judged and compensated or rewarded for their works. Our walk is centered around our position as sons/daughters of God and having a need to mature in Christ to receive the promise of heirship in Him. So, when we are positioned as sons/daughters of God in Christ, it means we are walking out our soul salvation and that we as children of God will be chastised by Him for sins committed prior to the rapture and us standing before the Judgment Seat of Christ. We must grow up in Christ to be qualified to inherit dominion in the Kingdom of God. Babes in Christ will not be allowed to take the reign of the Kingdom to exercise dominion and rule over nations. It simply will not happen because maturity solidifies character and in the Kingdom of God, character is highly revered.

"Now I say, That the heir, as long as he is a child, differeth nothing from a servant, though he be lord of all; But is under tutors and governors until the time appointed of the father. Even so we, when we were children, were in bondage under the elements of the world: But when the

fullness of the time was come, God sent forth his Son, made of a woman, made under the law, To redeem them that were under the law, that we might receive the adoption of sons. And because ye are sons, God hath sent forth the Spirit of his Son into your hearts, crying, Abba, Father. Wherefore thou art no more a servant, but a son; and if a son, then an heir of God through Christ." (Galations 4:1-7)

Maturing in Christ is a tedious and painstaking process that must be yielded to by believers. In fact, believers are indebted to Him and must grow in the knowledge and grace of Christ, since it was Jesus who purchased them on the cross at Cavalry. He is bringing in more sons/daughters to His Heavenly Father and it means that now being the offspring of the Father, they must also be chastised by Him whenever their free-will yields to sinful behavior. Those who find it hard to yield to the process of maturity will always be the ones walking around and looking over their shoulders in fear so to speak because in their immaturity, they have the inclination to test the boundaries of sin. But testing the boundaries of sin is dangerous and positions them for chastisement. Those who desire to move on to maturity in Christ will always govern their lives in such a way that they place a high value on their walk in Christ, and they have come to grips with the fact that this process to maturity will cost them everything.

"Wherefore, my beloved, as ye have always obeyed, not as in my presence only, but now much more in my absence, work out your own salvation with fear and trembling. For it is God which worketh in you both to will and to do of his good pleasure. Do all things without murmurings and disputings: That ye may be blameless and harmless, the sons of God, without rebuke, in the midst of a crooked and perverse nation, among whom ye shine as lights in the world." (Philippians 2:12-15)

Not only must believers mature in Christ, but they must also serve Him as faithful servants in all things. So, the first concept that believers must come to grips with is that anything the Lord entrusts them to accomplish is considered as work or an assignment. No matter how great or small the assignment might be, it is attributed to the work of the Lord. And if it is work done on His behalf, that means that He is your Boss or Lord; therefore, it is the Lord who will compensate or reward you for the labor that you have carried out for Him.

"For the kingdom of heaven is like unto a man that is an householder, which went out early in the morning to hire labourers into his vineyard. And when he had agreed with the labourers for a penny a day, he sent them into his vineyard. And he went out about the third hour, and saw

others standing idle in the marketplace, And said unto them; Go ye also into the vineyard, and whatsoever is right I will give you. And they went their way. Again he went out about the sixth and ninth hour, and did likewise. And about the eleventh hour he went out, and found others standing idle, and saith unto them, Why stand ye here all the day idle? They say unto him, Because no man hath hired us. He saith unto them, Go ye also into the vineyard; and whatsoever is right, that shall ye receive. So when even was come, the lord of the vineyard saith unto his steward, Call the labourers, and give them their hire, beginning from the last unto the first. And when they came that were hired about the eleventh hour, they received every man a penny. But when the first came, they supposed that they should have received more; and they likewise received every man a penny. And when they had received it, they murmured against the goodman of the house, Saying, These last have wrought but one hour, and thou hast made them equal unto us, which have borne the burden and heat of the day. But he answered one of them, and said, Friend, I do thee no wrong: didst not thou agree with me for a penny? Take that thine is, and go thy way: I will give unto this last, even as unto thee. Is it not lawful for me to do what I will with mine own? Is thine eye evil, because I am good?"
(Matthew 20:1-15)

Too many believers want instant gratification for the work they carry out in the name of the Lord. So, they boast and brag on their own accomplishment before the appointed time that has been set for the Lord to recompense them at the Judgment Seat of Christ. And they settle for much less than what the Lord had purposed for their reward or compensation. When they boast, they do it for a show to man, so that man can recompense them. To value the compensation of man over and above that of the Lord, is considered to be a distasteful thing to Him because the heart and motive behind the work is not based on pleasing the Lord, but rather based on promoting self in the eyesight of men. God deems such work as worthless and of little value in the Kingdom. He will not even consider the work to be worthy of compensation from Him, but rather it is considered to be a dead work that is not regarded as worthy of a reward at the Judgment Seat of Christ. You will have received your reward of labor from men.

"Take heed that ye do not your alms before men, to be seen of them: otherwise ye have no reward of your Father which is in heaven. Therefore when thou doest thine alms, do not sound a trumpet before thee, as the hypocrites do in the synagogues and in the streets, that they may have glory of men. Verily I say unto you, They have their reward. But when thou doest alms, let not thy left hand know what thy

right hand doeth: That thine alms may be in secret: and thy Father which seeth in secret himself shall reward thee openly." (Matthew 6:1-4)

Receiving rewards or compensation from Christ will differ greatly for believers. Everyone will not be worthy of the same measure and quality of compensation. So, every believer will not have the same degree of glory in their new resurrected bodies nor will they be accredited with the same ruling privileges or standings with the Lord. Many believers take the idea of being rewarded at the Judgment Seat of Christ very lightly. They do not seem to comprehend that many people will receive rewards, but even more will suffer loss of reward. And the loss of reward is a very grievous thing to bear when it is a decision based on the justice of God being served.

"But God giveth it a body as it hath pleased him, and to every seed his own body. All flesh is not the same flesh: but there is one kind of flesh of men, another flesh of beasts, another of fishes, and another of birds. There are also celestial bodies, and bodies terrestrial: but the glory of the celestial is one, and the glory of the terrestrial is another. There is one glory of the sun, and another glory of the moon, and another glory of the stars: for one star differeth from another star in glory. So also is the resurrection of the

dead. It is sown in corruption; it is raised in incorruption: It is sown in dishonour; it is raised in glory: it is sown in weakness; it is raised in power: It is sown a natural body; it is raised a spiritual body. There is a natural body, and there is a spiritual body." (I Corinthians 15:37-44)

Although all believers in Christ will stand at the Judgment Seat before Him because He paid the price for their sins on Calvary, not all will be able to rejoice in the same degree as others, seeing that they will suffer loss. They will suffer loss that will cause them to gnash their teeth knowing that they did not live up to God's standards on many occasions as it relates to their service to Him in this present time. Some will suffer the loss of loved ones, seeing that when they had the opportunity to minister Christ to them, they chose not to do so because they did not want to feel embarrassed in front of old friends and family members. Others will suffer loss because they were too greedy to sow financially to further the Kingdom of God on earth. They held back from God and chose rather to do things that satisfied their own desires. Then there will be those who suffer loss because they simply refused to keep clean hands and be sanctified wholly to God. So, we see that many believers will be in for a rude awakening at the Judgment Seat of Christ because they will see their Lord and Savior whom they have disappointed face to face. And they will no longer see Him in His role as the poor little lamb who was slain or the one who is currently interceding on their behalf. But they will see Him in the role of judge and experience the manner to which He righteously executes justice.

"Now he that planteth and he that watereth are one: and every man shall receive his own reward according to his own labour. For we are labourers together with God: ye are God's husbandry, ye are God's building. According to the grace of God which is given unto me, as a wise masterbuilder, I have laid the foundation, and another buildeth thereon. But let every man take heed how he buildeth thereupon. For other foundation can no man lay than that is laid, which is Jesus Christ. Now if any man build upon this foundation gold, silver, precious stones, wood, hay, stubble; Every man's work shall be made manifest: for the day shall declare it, because it shall be revealed by fire; and the fire shall try every man's work of what sort it is. If any man's work abide which he hath built thereupon, he shall receive a reward. If any man's work shall be burned, he shall suffer loss: but he himself shall be saved; yet so as by fire." (I Corinthians 3:8-15)

Standing at the Judgment Seat of Christ will be a beautiful and glorious event for those who have diligently prepared for such an occasion. But it shall be a very awkward and an intensely penetrating and shameful occurrence for believers who have been without anticipation of this great day. As believers, every day of our lives is a new day that affords us an opportunity to represent and magnify the Lord Jesus Christ in a world that knows Him not. Furthermore, believers are that light that shines in dark places and brings understanding to the darkened hearts and minds of men concerning the Lord and His Kingdom. If we do not shine as brilliant light in this world through our works on His behalf for whatever reason, when we stand at the Judgment Seat of Christ it will be a dreadful day because we must face our Lord who will expose everything about the intents of our hearts. Seeing that He is a just Lord, He will deal with us according to the condition of our hearts and caliber of our works, which is the very reason Apostles are always bent on trying to convince believers to not only be ready for that great day of judgment, but to be equally knowledgeable in the same. Meeting Jesus Christ as judge is completely different than His dealings with us in His roles of sacrificial lamb and mediator. These two roles allow us to understand the greater work of His grace, but the role of judge allows us to understand the strength and immutability of His word and righteousness. These factors surrounding the Lord Jesus Christ and the Kingdom simply cannot be compromised, no matter what. So, the Judgment Seat of Christ is a matter of monumental importance, as it will be decisive in judgment, life-altering in effects, and eternal in continuity. In other words, once the Lord settles His accounts with believers in that day, it will forever stand in the capacity that He has meted out.

"For we must all appear before the judgment seat of Christ; that every one may receive the things done in his body, according to that he hath done, whether it be good or bad. Knowing therefore the terror of the Lord, we persuade men; but we are made manifest unto God; and I trust also are made manifest in your consciences." (II Corinthians 5:10-11)

Cynthia Alvarez

Chapter 3
Judgment of Israel

The previous chapter gave us an overview of the Judgment Seat of Christ and revealed its characteristics that differ in many ways from succeeding judgments. We saw that not all believers will receive the same caliber of rewards and glory because the basis for judgment is their works. Everyone will not present the Lord with the same magnitude of work, so they will not all be equally compensated. It is similar to Cain and Abel when they presented God with a sacrifice from the labor of their own hands. They did not receive the same affirmation from God. Cain's offering did not measure up to His standards in the same capacity that Abel's offering did. Cain knew that God was not pleased with the labor of his hands and to see God accept Abel's labor as a work of excellence was disheartening to him. In fact, it was a day of shame and dishonor for Cain that has been recorded throughout history as a testimony of the eternal value that is attached to the labor of all believers.

"And in process of time it came to pass, that Cain brought of the fruit of the ground an offering unto the LORD. And Abel, he also brought of the firstlings of his flock and of the fat

thereof. And the LORD had respect unto Abel and to his offering: But unto Cain and to his offering he had not respect. And Cain was very wroth, and his countenance fell. And the LORD said unto Cain, Why art thou wroth? and why is thy countenance fallen? If thou doest well, shalt thou not be accepted? and if thou doest not well, sin lieth at the door. And unto thee shall be his desire, and thou shalt rule over him." (Genesis 4: 3-7)

The Judgment Seat of Christ is truly a glorious and frightening event for all believers appointed to it. Preparation is key. Those who are prepared to stand in that day will be crowned with glory and those who are not prepared, will know the futility of their labor.

After we move forward in examining the five different judgments of God, we turn to the next judgment that centers around Israel, which is commonly known as the Judgment of Israel or the 'Time of Jacob's Trouble'. It is viewed in such terms because it will be the darkest and most troubling hour in the history of this nation. It is when wrath is unleashed upon Israel for their transgressions and blatant rejection of the entire Godhead. Throughout the history of the nation of Israel, we have seen that God for the most part has dealt with chastising Israel through the gentile nations that rose up against them. Whenever Israel turned away from God in disobedience, God would allow the gentiles the privilege of prevailing over them. Why? Because God had to make them understand that it was by His hand that they were blessed and victorious over all the nations on earth, as God had purposed Israel to be the head of the nations or the superpower nation on earth.

"Now these are the nations which the LORD left, to prove Israel by them, even as many of Israel as had not known all the wars of Canaan; Only that the generations of the children of Israel might know, to teach them war, at the least such as before knew nothing thereof; Namely, five lords of the Philistines, and all the Canaanites, and the Sidonians, and the Hivites that dwelt in mount Lebanon, from mount Baalhermon unto the entering in of Hamath. And they were to prove Israel by them, to know whether they would hearken unto the commandments of the LORD, which he commanded their fathers by the hand of Moses. And the children of Israel dwelt among the Canaanites, Hittites, and Amorites, and Perizzites, and Hivites, and Jebusites: And they took their daughters to be their wives, and gave their daughters to their sons, and served their gods. And the children of Israel did evil in the sight of the LORD, and forgat the LORD their God, and served Baalim and the groves. Therefore the anger of the LORD was hot against Israel, and he sold them into the hand of

Chushanrishathaim king of Mesopotamia: and the children of Israel served Chushanrishathaim eight years. And when the children of Israel cried unto the LORD, the LORD raised up a deliverer to the children of Israel, who delivered them, even Othniel the son of Kenaz, Caleb's younger brother." (Judges 3:1-9)

Yet, Israel's rejection of the Godhead in total throughout their existence on earth has warranted judgment. The word of God makes it clear that Israel did not want to be ruled over by God the Father, God the Son, or God the Holy Spirit. But we must first comprehend when viewing the Judgment of Israel is that unlike the Church, which is engaged to Jesus at this current time, Israel is already married to God the Father. This marriage took place in the Old Testament. The Church does not become the wife of Jesus until the marriage supper of the Lamb takes place after the rapture. But Israel is a wife and not a virgin who is engaged. Although she has played the harlot among the nations, she is the wife of the Almighty God.

Israel is the wife of God the Father

"For thy Maker is thing husband; the LORD of hosts is his name; and thy Redeemer the Holy One of Israel; The God of the whole earth shall he be called. For the LORD hath called thee as a woman forsaken and grieved in spirit, and a wife of youth,

when thou wast refused, saith thy God. For a small moment have I forsaken thee; but with great mercies will I gather thee." (Isaiah 54:5-7)

The Church is engaged to Jesus Christ

"For I am jealous over you with godly jealousy: for I have espoused you to one husband, that I may present you as a chaste virgin to Christ." (II Corinthians 11:2)

When we understand the standing of Israel with God the Father and the standing of the Church with Jesus Christ, the varying degrees of their judgments makes more sense. Being a wife is much different than being engaged. To be a wife means to be in covenant with a husband, whereas being engaged means that a covenant is pending validation until the marriage is official. So, whenever Israel as a wife would commit adultery by worshipping other gods and rejecting God the Father, she sinned against her very own husband. She violated their marriage covenant. But whenever those in the Church sin against Jesus, it is considered fornication, and they instead sin against their own body and do it to their own detriment because the marriage between the Church and Jesus is not consummated until the marriage supper of the Lamb takes place. The down payment of the Holy Ghost is the token of the promise of an espousal between the Lord and His Church.

Israel Rejects God the Father
The Father marries Israel at Mt. Sinai

"Now therefore, if ye will obey my voice indeed, and keep my covenant, then ye shall be a peculiar treasure unto me above all people: for all the earth is mine: And ye shall be unto me a kingdom of priests, and an holy nation. These are the words which thou shalt speak unto the children of Israel. And Moses came and called for the elders of the people, and laid before their faces all these words which the LORD commanded him. And all the people answered together, and said, all that the LORD hath spoken we will do. And Moses returned the words of the people unto the LORD." (Exodus 19:5-8)

When reading the scriptures in Exodus of the marriage between God the Father and Israel, it shows the character of the traditional marriage vows between a man and woman. It is a binding covenant that is rooted in love and faithfulness. Exodus chapter 19 details the marriage in love and Exodus chapter 20 chronicles what Israel must be 100% faithful or loyal in doing as a wife who honors her husband. These wifely duties were the sum-total of the ten commandments. Her husband (God the Father) had made known to her the only manner of which she can genuinely show her faithfulness or loyalty to Him in this marriage covenant, was by fully honoring His revealed will encompassed in those ten commandments. By this, she would prove to be virtuous and praiseworthy as the wife of one man (One God).

Ten Commandments – (Exodus Chapter 20)

1. Thou shalt have no other gods before me.
2. Thou shalt not make unto thee any graven image, or any likeness of anything that is in heaven above, or that is in the earth beneath, or that is in the water under the earth.
3. Thou shalt not take the name of the Lord thy God in vain.
4. Remember the sabbath day, to keep it holy.
5. Honor thy father and thy mother: that thy days may be long upon the land which the Lord thy God giveth thee.
6. Thou shalt not kill.
7. Thou shalt not commit adultery.
8. Thou shalt not steal
9. Thou shalt not bear false witness against thy brother.
10. Thou shall not covet thy neighbor's house, thou shalt not covet thy neighbor's wife, nor his manservant, nor his maidservant, nor his ox, nor his ass, nor anything that is thy neighbor's.

Although given these terms of the marriage covenant, Israel's history of disobedience and unfaithfulness was long and repetitive. Yet, God was longsuffering with her and attempted time and time again to bring her heart back to Him. Instead of turning to Him with her whole heart, she rejected the very thought of Him ruling over her. Israel wanted a different kind of king ruling over her. She wanted what all the nations whom she committed adultery with had, a king that looked like them. Someone they could relate to on their own level. Israel had grown tired of a God/King that was not their equal, and so they demanded that they were given such a king. It was open and blatant rejection of the Father God by His wife.

"Then all the elders of Israel gathered themselves together, and came to Samuel unto Ramah, And said unto him, Behold, thou art old, and thy sons walk not in thy ways: now make us a king to judge us like all the nations. But the thing displeased Samuel, when they said, Give us a king to judge us. And Samuel prayed unto the LORD. And the LORD said unto Samuel, Hearken unto the voice of the people in all that they say unto thee: for they have not rejected thee, but they have rejected me, that I should not reign over them." (I Samuel 8:4-7)

The constant adultery and betrayal of Israel against the Father God finally reached a climax, and He gave her His official divorce papers. Notwithstanding, He will not cast her off or put her away forever. In fact, He has plans to gather her to Himself once again after the Great Tribulation judgment. More details of the Great Tribulation will be discussed later in this chapter, so that I do not get ahead of myself concerning the Judgment of Israel.

"And I saw, when for all the causes whereby backsliding Israel committed adultery I had put her away, and given her a bill of divorce; yet her treacherous sister Judah feared not, but went and played the harlot also." (Jeremiah 3:8)

Israel Rejects God the Son

Israel's rejection of Jesus (God the Son) is not without expectation, since they had so long ago rejected God the Father. Her rejection of God the Father as husband, led to Him serving them divorce papers. In addition, He also allowed the Gentile nations to rise to dominion over Israel, which is commonly known as 'The Times of the Gentiles'. As the wife of God, Israel was to be the head of the nations or the superpower nation in the earth. She would represent God the Father upon the earth and all nations would have to turn to Israel to learn about the Almighty God and Creator. But after Israel rejected God the Father from being her king, He had to allow her to experience what living without God as her king would be like. It would resemble hell on earth. It would mean that she would have to see Gentile nations rise to dominion over her time and time again. There would be no more visions to direct Israel in reaching the glorious destiny that many of the prophets spoke of in the Old Testament. They would be scattered throughout the Gentile nations and many would lose their national identity. In this state of being without a king and the consequences that followed, caused Israel to be in dire need of a deliverer. Although they received no new visions, they still held to the prophecies that were given by many of the Old Testament prophets. These prophecies spoke of a glorious destiny for Israel and a Messiah who would one day come and deliver them from the rule of Gentile nations and restore the nation to its rightful place as head of the nations in the Kingdom. The Gentiles rise to power and dominion can be seen with Nebuchadnezzar's statue in the book of Daniel.

"Thou, O king, sawest, and behold a great image. This great image, whose brightness was excellent, stood before thee; and the form thereof was terrible.
This image's head was of fine gold, his breast and his arms of silver, his belly and his thighs of brass, His legs of iron, his feet part of iron and part of clay. Thou sawest till that a

stone was cut out without hands, which smote the image upon his feet that were of iron and clay, and brake them to pieces. Then was the iron, the clay, the brass, the silver, and the gold, broken to pieces together, and became like the chaff of the summer threshingfloors; and the wind carried them away, that no place was found for them: and the stone that smote the image became a great mountain, and filled the whole earth. This is the dream; and we will tell the interpretation thereof before the king. Thou, O king, art a king of kings: for the God of heaven hath given thee a kingdom, power, and strength, and glory. And wheresoever the children of men dwell, the beasts of the field and the fowls of the heaven hath he given into thine hand, and hath made thee ruler over them all. Thou art this head of gold. And after thee shall arise another kingdom inferior to thee, and another third kingdom of brass, which shall bear rule over all the earth. And the fourth kingdom shall be strong as iron: forasmuch as iron breaketh in pieces and subdueth all things: and as iron that breaketh all these, shall it break in pieces and bruise. And whereas thou sawest the feet and toes, part of potters' clay, and part of iron, the kingdom shall be divided; but there shall be in it of the strength of the iron, forasmuch as thou sawest the iron mixed with miry clay. And as the toes of the feet were part of iron, and part of clay, so the kingdom shall be partly strong, and partly broken. And whereas thou sawest iron mixed with miry clay, they shall mingle themselves with the seed of men: but they shall not cleave one to another, even as iron is not mixed with clay. And in the days of these kings shall the God of heaven set up a kingdom, which shall never be destroyed: and the kingdom shall not be left to other people, but it shall break in pieces and consume all these kingdoms, and it shall stand forever." (Daniel 2:31-44)

Because Israel had not seen the fulfillment of prophecies regarding her glorious days at any point during the Times of the Gentiles, she continued to look for the promised Messiah (Deliverer) that was spoken of by the prophets of old. So, Israel's response to Jesus' first coming was quite contrary to what was appropriate for the arrival of her long-awaited king. Israel was looking for the lion of the tribe of Judah to appear on the scene, but Jesus came as a lamb and lowly servant. Israel did not understand Jesus in this role as a lamb because the bulk of prophecies that she had received in the Old Testament centered around a Messiah who would come as King of Kings and Lord of Lords. Israel had certain expectations of her Messiah and Jesus did not fit the picture she had envisioned. At the least, she wanted to see a King in the similitude of her great earthly King David, who was a man after God's own heart. David was a warrior, a man of wisdom, and beloved by all of Israel. As such, she anticipated a king and deliverer who would come on the scene and immediately put his efforts into establishing the Kingdom of Israel to her rightful place as head of the nations. And to lay eyes on a weak and lowly servant who came in the name of the Almighty God of Israel was unacceptable. Israel had no reservations about making her disappointment known openly. She refused Jesus as King and petitioned for Him to receive the death penalty, since He was unfit to do anything to bring about the physical establishment of the Kingdom as head of the nations. Collectively, she requested the death of Jesus and the pardoning of Barrabas, who was a well-known political activist of establishing the Kingdom. Israel felt that she stood a better chance of realizing her desire in seeing the Kingdom come into fuition with Barrabas than she ever would with Jesus. She refused to allow such a lowly and unaccomplished person to rule over her, even if it meant sentencing an innocent man to death.

"And they cried out all at once, saying, Away with this man, and release unto us Barabbas: (Who for a certain sedition made in the city, and for murder, was cast into prison.) Pilate therefore, willing to release Jesus, spake again to them. But they cried, saying, Crucify him, crucify him. And he said unto them the third time, Why, what evil hath he done? I have found no cause of death in him: I will therefore chastise him, and let him go. And they were instant with

loud voices, requiring that he might be crucified. And the voices of them and of the chief priests prevailed. And Pilate gave sentence that it should be as they required." (Luke 23:18-24)

Israel Rejects God the Holy Spirit

We see that when Jesus appeared, He did not come to establish the Kingdom in physical form at that moment, yet He came to re-establish the heart of Israel to God the Father once again. This was necessary and had to precede a physical manifestation of the Kingdom because Jesus being God, understood that the basis of the Kingdom of Israel being physically established forever on earth is based on righteous men living righteous lives in a righteous Kingdom. This could not happen apart from the heart of Israel being converted prior to the commencement of the glorious Kingdom Age or Millennial Age.

"A new heart also will I give you, and a new spirit will I put within you: and I will take away the stony heart out of your flesh, and I will give you an heart of flesh. And I will put my spirit within you, and cause you to walk in my statutes, and ye shall keep my judgments, and do them. And ye shall dwell in the land that I gave to your fathers; and ye shall be my people, and I will be your God." (Ezekiel 36:26-28)

"Jesus answered and said unto him, Verily, verily, I say unto thee, except a man be born again, he cannot see the kingdom of God." (John 3:3)

When Jesus came to Israel, He knew that she would reject Him. It was not a surprise to Him in the same sense that it was to everyone else. Jesus came as a lamb and lowly servant because He had to pay the penalty for the sin of humanity, so that He could purchase a bride or Church for Himself. And this bride is His queen who will rule and reign with Jesus during the Kingdom Age or Millennial Age. The Kingdom would not commence without His co-regent bride or Church. The Church was a mystery that was hid in Christ before the foundation of the world. It had not been revealed in the Old Testament. In fact, it was Apostle Paul who was chosen to reveal the mystery of the Church of God in Christ Jesus.

"But I certify you, brethren, that the gospel which was preached of me is not after man.
For I neither received it of man, neither was I taught it, but by the revelation of Jesus Christ. For ye have heard of my conversation in time past in the Jews' religion, how that beyond measure I persecuted the church of God, and wasted it: And profited in the Jews' religion above many my equals in mine own nation, being more exceedingly zealous of the traditions of my fathers. But when it pleased God, who

separated me from my mother's womb, and called me by his grace." (Galatians 1:11-16)

The Church is a new creation in Christ, and if she is in Christ, she must be filled with the same substance or spirit that Christ has. It is impossible to be a member of His Church and not be indwelled by His Spirit.

"But ye are not in the flesh, but in the Spirit, if so be that the Spirit of God dwell in you. Now if any man have not the Spirit of Christ, he is none of his." (Romans 8:9)

This is the same message that Stephen tried to make known to Israel, but she refused it because his words pricked her heart. Israel was only concerned with establishing and restoring the Kingdom to its rightful place. She had not heard of a Holy Spirit and thought this was the work of the devil. Because of her hardened heart, Stephen made her spiritual condition known through his preaching. But Israel was angered by such speech concerning her and this absurd talk of a Holy Spirit. So, she reverted to silencing Stephen by stoning him to death. In doing so, she fully rejected God the Holy Spirit.

"When they heard these things, they were cut to the heart, and they gnashed on him with their teeth. But he, being full of the Holy Ghost, looked up steadfastly into heaven, and

saw the glory of God, and Jesus standing on the right hand of God, And said, Behold, I see the heavens opened, and the Son of man standing on the right hand of God. Then they cried out with a loud voice, and stopped their ears, and ran upon him with one accord, And cast him out of the city, and stoned him: and the witnesses laid down their clothes at a young man's feet, whose name was Saul. And they stoned Stephen, calling upon God, and saying, Lord Jesus, receive my spirit. And he kneeled down, and cried with a loud voice, Lord, lay not this sin to their charge. And when he had said this, he fell asleep." (Acts 7:54-60)

In a haste to silence Stephen, Israel prevented the ministry work of the Holy Spirit from going forth on a national scale. She forfeited the opportunity to be converted as a nation by the Holy Spirit. Because of her offensive actions towards the Holy Spirit, God suspended His dealings with her for over 2,000 years, except a small number or a small remnant of Israel that believed and received the Holy Spirit. God turned to the Gentile nations during this time that Israel rejected the Holy Spirit and it is known as the Age of Grace. During this age, His unmerited favor in shed abroad in the hearts of all believers in Christ. It is during this age that Gentiles were given the opportunity to receive the gift of the Holy Spirit and become part of the new creation in Christ, which is the Church. Therefore, more gentiles than Israelites will make up the glorious Church of Christ and will rule and reign with Him in the Kingdom or Millennial Age.

"Whereby, when ye read, ye may understand my knowledge in the mystery of Christ." (Ephesians 3:4-6)

We must keep the severity of Israel's rejection of the entire Godhead at the forefront as the basis of her judgment. For the magnitude of her sins, she has been appointed to wrath. It is the 'Time of Jacob's Trouble' and it is a time of dread for her. In fact, it is the only way that Israel will realize the greatness of her sin against God and turn to repentance. Without repentance, she can never be restored to being head of the nations. And if she is not in position as the head of the nations, we cannot move into the Kingdom Age or Millennial Age because this glorious age rests on the basis of Israel being the head and not the tail of the nations. Therefore, God will allow the judgment of Israel to be consummated through chastisement at the hand of the Anti-Christ, who will be the head of the last Gentile reign over Israel. During this time of judgment, the Anti-Christ will gather a ten-nation federation or alliance and seek to destroy the nation of Israel in great wrath.

"And the ten horns out of this kingdom are ten kings that shall arise: and another shall rise after them; and he shall be diverse from the first, and he shall subdue

three kings. And he shall speak great words against the most High, and shall wear out the saints of the most High, and think to change times and laws: and they shall be given into his hand until a time and times and the dividing of time." (Daniel 7:24-25)

His hatred for Israel will be unrelenting because the Anti-Christ will be Satan incarnate or in the flesh. So, he is fully aware of Israel being God's nation and all the glorious prophecies that pertain to Israel's glorious reign in the Kingdom Age or Millennial Age with Jesus as King of Kings and Lord of Lords ruling from the throne in Jerusalem. Satan's goal is to seize that throne, destroy the nation of Israel, and usher in his own Millennial Age that excludes the Lord Jesus Christ and Israel. In fact, he will attempt to destroy them both, since his agenda still houses the same plans that caused his rebellion in heaven eons ago. Satan in the form of the Anti-Christ still wants to take possession of the throne of God for himself.

"How art thou fallen from heaven, O Lucifer, son of the morning! how art thou cut down to the ground, which didst weaken the nations! For thou hast said in thine heart, I will ascend into heaven, I will exalt my throne above the stars of God: I will sit also upon the mount of the congregation, in

the sides of the north: I will ascend above the heights of the clouds; I will be like the most High." (Isaiah 14:12-14)

Although Satan as the Anti-Christ will attempt to seize the throne of God in rebellion once again, the outcome of his treachery remains the same, he will utterly fail. God is not intimidated or moved by Satan's antics, especially when the Lord Jesus Christ is the rightful King and heir to the throne of glory in Jerusalem. Again, Satan utterly fails.

"Yet thou shalt be brought down to hell, to the sides of the pit. They that see thee shall narrowly look upon thee, and consider thee, saying, Is this the man that made the earth to tremble, that did shake kingdoms; That made the world as a wilderness, and destroyed the cities thereof; that opened not the house of his prisoners?"
(Isaiah 14:15-17)

But Satan as the Anti-Christ does not fail without chastising Israel according to the judgment of God. Israel will flee for her life from the hand of the Anti-Christ into neighboring countries and will find a place of safety in the wilderness that has been prepared for her by God. She will be in this safe haven when the Lord Jesus Christ will return from heaven for every eye to see Him. And it will be at this time that Israel will recognize Him as their Messiah and realize what they had done in crucifying Him.

"And I will pour upon the house of David, and upon the inhabitants of Jerusalem, the spirit of grace and of supplications: and they shall look upon me whom they have pierced, and they shall mourn for him, as one mourneth for his only son, and shall be in bitterness for him, as one that is in bitterness for his firstborn." (Zechariah 12:9-10)

Israel will be sorrowful to the point of repentance and will be converted as a nation at that time. She will receive her long-awaited King, as He takes up His rightful place on the throne of His glory in Jerusalem. It will be at this moment that Israel will see the fulfillment of prophecy concerning the restoration of the Kingdom of Israel, which will move the earth into the glorious Kingdom Age.

Cynthia Alvarez

Chapter 4
Judgment of the Nations

In Chapter Three, we were able to analyze the Judgment of Israel and understand the reasoning behind the intense chastisement that has been appointed to the nation based on their willful rejection of the entire Godhead. Israel rejected God the Father as her husband in the Old Testament. In the New Testament, Israel rejected Jesus as her Messiah and rejected receiving the inner dwelling of the Holy Spirit that would have given her a new nature or new heart. She committed adultery against her husband, God the Father and demanded the death of her Messiah. Then she rejected the gift of the Holy Spirit and stoned Stephen to death because he spoke in the authority of the Spirit concerning Israel's sin against God. Israel wanted no parts of God at all. And so, we see that the judgment that is dealt to her, is just and righteous to the converting of the entire nation at once. No more will she play the harlot among the nations, but she will take her rightful place as head of the nations.

"And the LORD shall make thee the head, and not the tail; and thou shalt be above only, and thou shalt not be beneath;

if that thou hearken unto the commandments of the LORD thy God, which I command thee this day, to observe and to do them." (Deuteronomy 28:13)

If Israel is to be head of the nations, we must understand the overall condition of these nations that warranted the need for Israel to rule over them. The nations of the world were estranged from God because they were under the rule of fallen angels and demons. Having no way to associate with Him, they were spiritually lost and blind. So, they served the gods or fallen angels that were known to them through religious rituals that served the purpose of binding them to such gods.

"But I say, that the things which the Gentiles sacrifice, they sacrifice to devils, and not to God: and I would not that ye should have fellowship with devils." (I Corinthians 10:20)

So, when dealing with these nations at any level, it means that you must also deal with the gods or fallen angels that exercise authority over them. Whether you are in alliance with these nations, going to war against these nations, or simply intermingling through marriage with those within these nations, you will come in contact with their gods to some degree. But God's plan for humanity included the nations of the world too because He loves mankind. When God chose Israel and formed them, He did so with purpose in mind. Israel would be made to be the head of nations, which meant that they would be the nation that led other nations to God. Through Israel, the nations would learn about God and His laws, so that they would no longer be estranged from their creator and God. Yet, Israel's constant sinning and backsliding throughout the old testament frustrated the purpose of God. They had to be judged and the nations remained estranged from God. Israel received judgment of 490 years to be chastised at the hand of God through the Gentile nations. This meant that Israel would not be able to rise to the glorious status as head of the nations until the 490 years of chastisement had been completed. The prophet Daniel was the human vessel who received the words of this dreary judgment upon his people from the angel Gabriel. It was a decree that could not be overturned because it was irrevocable in every way. The decree originated in heaven from the throne of God and was executed on earth, not the other way around.

"Yea, whiles I was speaking in prayer, even the man Gabriel, whom I had seen in the vision at the beginning, being caused to fly swiftly, touched me about the time of the evening oblation. And he informed me, and talked with me, and said, O Daniel, I am now come forth to give thee skill

and understanding. At the beginning of thy supplications the commandment came forth, and I am come to shew thee; for thou art greatly beloved: therefore understand the matter, and consider the vision.

Seventy weeks are determined upon thy people and upon thy holy city, to finish the transgression, and to make an end of sins, and to make reconciliation for iniquity, and to bring in everlasting righteousness, and to seal up the vision and prophecy, and to anoint the most Holy." (Daniel 9:21-24)

Because this judgment prevented Israel from taking her rightful place as head of the nations for the span of 490 years, the 'Times of the Gentiles' came to the forefront. Which means that instead of Israel being the leading nation, gentile nations rose up and became the dominant powers in succession throughout the years appointed for Israel's judgment. Yes, Israel became the more inferior nation to the rising gentile nations, with the first of the gentile nations to rise in great power after the decree was made known to Daniel was Babylon. The rise of Babylon and the succession of gentile nations throughout the 490 years is seen in the dream that Nebuchadnezzar had regarding an image or statue that was shown to him, in which Daniel explained the details of the image or statue being a prophetic account of

The Judgments of God

the ruling gentile nations during the length of Israel's judgment.

'The king answered and said to Daniel, whose name was Belteshazzar, Art thou able to make known unto me the dream which I have seen, and the interpretation thereof? Daniel answered in the presence of the king, and said, The secret which the king hath demanded cannot the wise men, the astrologers, the magicians, the soothsayers, shew unto the king; But there is a God in heaven that revealeth secrets, and maketh known to the king Nebuchadnezzar what shall be in the latter days. Thy dream, and the visions of thy head upon thy bed, are these; As for thee, O king, thy thoughts came into thy mind upon thy bed, what should come to pass hereafter: and he that revealeth secrets maketh known to thee what shall come to pass. But as for me, this secret is not revealed to me for any wisdom that I have more than any living, but for their sakes that shall make known the interpretation to the king, and that thou mightest know the thoughts of thy heart. Thou, O king, sawest, and behold a great image. This great image, whose brightness was excellent, stood before thee; and the form thereof was terrible. This image's head was of fine gold, his breast and his arms of silver, his belly and his thighs of brass, His legs of iron, his feet part of iron and part of clay. Thou sawest till that a stone was cut

out without hands, which smote the image upon his feet that were of iron and clay, and brake them to pieces. Then was the iron, the clay, the brass, the silver, and the gold, broken to pieces together, and became like the chaff of the summer threshingfloors; and the wind carried them away, that no place was found for them: and the stone that smote the image became a great mountain and filled the whole earth." (Daniel 2: 26-35)

The gentile nations which came to the forefront of dominion in that vicinity of the earth during this time have been Babylon, Persia, Greece, and Rome. And each of these nations makes up a division or a segment of the image that Nebuchadnezzar saw. Israel was taken into captivity time after time by these nations because of sin and disobedience. But when she would repent and turn back to God, a remnant was always allowed to return to the land of Israel. When Jesus left glory as the lamb of God, Israel was under Roman dominion and only had 7 years left from the 490 years of judgment that was appointed to the nation. But when Israel rejected Jesus as their Messiah and crucified Him, they were left in an unrepented position. God in all grace offered her the gift of the Holy Spirit if she would repent, so that He could dwell in her through His Spirt. But Israel violently rejected the Holy Spirit too. At this point, God suspended

His dealings with the nation of Israel and turned His attention to the gentiles and proceeded to do a new thing. With the nation of Israel being in an unrepentant position and having rejected the entire Godhead, she was basically on equal standing at that point with the gentile nations who were estranged from God. In this standing, God had leveled the playing field and made it possible to offer salvation to both Israel and the gentiles, while making them a new creation in Christ.

"Even the righteousness of God which is by faith of Jesus Christ unto all and upon all them that believe: for there is no difference: For all have sinned, and come short of the glory of God; Being justified freely by his grace through the redemption that is in Christ Jesus. Whom God hath set forth to be a propitiation through faith in his blood, to declare his righteousness for the remission of sins that are past, through the forbearance of God; To declare, I say, at this time his righteousness: that he might be just, and the justifier of him which believeth in Jesus. Where is boasting then? It is excluded. By what law? of works? Nay: but by the law of faith. Therefore we conclude that a man is justified by faith without the deeds of the law. Is he the God of the Jews only? is he not also of the Gentiles? Yes, of the Gentiles also." (Romans 3:22-29)

So, we see that we are currently living in this era where God has suspended His dealing with Israel as it relates to her judgment and being restored to head of the nations. As we have seen, this suspension is now over 2,000 years in duration, so that the gentiles too can partake of His loving generosity in this Age of Grace and that the principality or powers in heavenly places can also witness to the unrestrained wisdom of God towards humanity. Once God completes His demonstration of grace and wisdom through His new creation, the Church, He will rapture and receive the Church to Himself.

"And to make all men see what is the fellowship of the mystery, which from the beginning of the world hath been hid in God, who created all things by Jesus Christ: to the intent that now unto the principalities and powers in heavenly places might be known by the church the manifold wisdom of God." (Ephesians 3:9-10)

After the Church has been raptured, God will commence His dealings with Israel to complete the final 7 years of the 490 years of judgment appointed to the nation. So once again, Gentile rule must be at the forefront. We will see this take place as the Anti-Christ comes on the scene and brings forth a ten-nation federation or alliance of gentiles who will have a common agenda. This agenda will be the annihilation of nation of Israel, the Anti-Christ becoming supreme ruler of the world by possessing the throne of glory in Jerusalem.

"And the ten horns which thou sawest are ten kings, which have received no kingdom as yet; but receive power as kings one hour with the beast. These have one mind, and shall give their power and strength unto the beast. These shall make war with the Lamb, and the Lamb shall overcome them: for he is Lord of lords, and King of kings: and they that are with him are called, and chosen, and faithful." (Revelation 17:12-14)

During this tumultuous time, the nation of Israel shall be persecuted by the Anti-Christ after he breaks a peace treaty with her during the latter part of the Tribulation, which is known as the Great Tribulation. At the onset of the Great Tribulation, the Anti-Christ will suffer a mortal wound, but will be supernaturally healed and many people will be deceived by this wonder and will worship him as God. It is widely believed that because he will be a powerful political leader, this wound will be the result of an assassination attempt against his life. When the Anti-Christ suffers this mortal wound, it is then that Satan shall be incarnated within him to take full possession of his body, as we see the striking difference in his character before the mortal wound happens and after he is healed from the wound. There is a drastic and extremely dark change that takes place concerning him. He violates the peace treaty and sets out to destroy the nation of Israel and all who oppose him. These events are clearly detailed in the books of Daniel and Revelation.

Anti-Christ as detailed in the book of Daniel

"And in the latter time of their kingdom, when the transgressors are come to the full, a king of fierce countenance, and understanding dark sentences, shall stand up. And his power shall be mighty, but not by his own power: and he shall destroy wonderfully, and shall prosper, and practice, and shall destroy the mighty and the holy people. And through his policy also he shall cause craft to prosper in his hand; and he shall magnify himself in his heart, and by peace shall destroy many: he shall also stand up against the Prince of princes; but he shall be broken without hand." (Daniel 8:23-25)

Anti-Christ as detailed in the book of Revelation

"And the beast which I saw was like unto a leopard, and his feet were as the feet of a bear, and his mouth as the mouth of a lion: and the dragon gave him his power, and his seat,

and great authority. And I saw one of his heads as it were wounded to death; and his deadly wound was healed: and all the world wondered after the beast. And they worshipped the dragon which gave power unto the beast: and they worshipped the beast, saying, Who is like unto the beast? who is able to make war with him? And there was given unto him a mouth speaking great things and blasphemies; and power was given unto him to continue forty and two months. And he opened his mouth in blasphemy against God, to blaspheme his name, and his tabernacle, and them that dwell in heaven. And it was given unto him to make war with the saints, and to overcome them: and power was given him over all kindreds, and tongues, and nations. And all that dwell upon the earth shall worship him, whose names are not written in the book of life of the Lamb slain from the foundation of the world." (Revelation 13:2-8)

As the Anti-Christ turns his wrath on the nation of Israel, she will flee for her life to other nations, even into the wilderness. And when she flees to certain nations during the Great Tribulation, she will experience rejection and will be ill-treated. But there will be other nations that will welcome her and nourish her during this horrific time. She will find safety in the wilderness because God will have prepared a place and safe haven for her to flee to that will provide protection against the wrath of the Anti-Christ. It is at this time that Jesus Christ will return in the clouds of heaven for every eye to see Him. He will destroy the Anti-Christ and his armies with the sword of his mouth. Israel will see Him and understand that Jesus Christ is their Messiah whom they crucified at His first coming.

"And I saw heaven opened and behold a white horse; and he that sat upon him was called Faithful and True, and in righteousness he doth judge and make war. His eyes were as a flame of fire, and on his head were many crowns; and he had a name written, that no man knew, but he himself. And he was clothed with a vesture dipped in blood: and his name is called The Word of God. And the armies which were in heaven followed him upon white horses, clothed in fine linen, white and clean. And out of his mouth goeth a sharp sword, that with it he should smite the nations: and he shall rule them with a rod of iron: and he treadeth the winepress of the fierceness and wrath of Almighty God. And he hath on his vesture and on his thigh a name written, KING OF KINGS, AND LORD OF LORDS. And I saw an angel standing in the sun; and he cried with a loud voice, saying to all the fowls that fly in the midst of heaven, Come and gather yourselves together unto the supper of the great God; That ye may eat the flesh of kings, and the flesh of captains, and the flesh of mighty men, and

the flesh of horses, and of them that sit on them, and the flesh of all men, both free and bond, both small and great. And I saw the beast, and the kings of the earth, and their armies, gathered together to make war against him that sat on the horse, and against his army. And the beast was taken, and with him the false prophet that wrought miracles before him, with which he deceived them that had received the mark of the beast, and them that worshipped his image. These both were cast alive into a lake of fire burning with brimstone. And the remnant were slain with the sword of him that sat upon the horse, which sword proceeded out of his mouth: and all the fowls were filled with their flesh." (Revelation 19:11-21)

Upon His arrival, Jesus will destroy the armies of the Anti-Christ and cast this wicked ruler into the lake of fire. As for Satan, he will be bound and cast into the bottomless pit for the span of 1000 years. He will have no access to the world, nor will he have influence over the cultures of the world. The Lord will at this point recover the spheres that influence all cultures of the world. His dominion will be global; therefore, the culture of the Kingdom will spread across the entire planet. Not in some places, but in all places.

"And I saw an angel come down from heaven, having the key of the bottomless pit and a great chain in his hand. And

he laid hold on the dragon, that old serpent, which is the Devil, and Satan, and bound him a thousand years, and cast him into the bottomless pit, and shut him up, and set a seal upon him, that he should deceive the nations no more, till the thousand years should be fulfilled: and after that he must be loosed a little season." (Revelation 20:1-3)

The dramatic revelation of Jesus Christ being the true Messiah of Israel will cause her to repent and be converted as a nation, which will bring the last week or last seven years of her appointed judgment to an end. She will have endured 490 years of judgment as a nation for her transgressions and rejection of the Godhead. And she will now be able to be restored to her rightful place as head of the nations on earth, with Jesus Christ ruling in her midst on the throne of His glory in Jerusalem to usher in the Kingdom Age or Millennial Age. Yet, the Kingdom Age will not commence until Jesus judges the nations of the earth to determine which nations will be allowed to enter the Kingdom Age and the nations that will be denied entrance into the Kingdom Age. The nations denied entrance will be condemned to everlasting punishment. The sole basis of this great judgment of the nations is their treatment of the nation of Israel during the Tribulation or the last week of her appointed judgment. The nations who had pity and treated her kind, will be rewarded with life in the Kingdom Age. Those nations that took advantage of the opportunity to kick Israel when she was down and enduring the chastisement of the Lord, will be barred from the Kingdom Age and appointed everlasting punishment. So, we see that the judgment of nations immediately precedes the commencement of the glorious Kingdom Age. Not only does the Kingdom Age commence, but the Times of the Gentiles or gentile dominion comes to an end. The Kingdom of God will be manifested for all to see and Jesus will rule as Sovereign King. He will have received His long-awaited kingdom.

"When the Son of man shall come in his glory, and all the holy angels with him, then shall he sit upon the throne of his glory: And before him shall be gathered all nations: and he shall separate them one from another, as a shepherd divideth his sheep from the goats: And he shall set the sheep on his right hand, but the goats on the left. Then shall the King say unto them on his right hand, Come, ye blessed of my Father, inherit the kingdom prepared for you from the foundation of the world: For I was an hungred, and ye gave me meat: I was thirsty, and ye gave me drink: I was a stranger, and ye took me in: Naked, and ye clothed me: I was sick, and ye visited me: I was in prison, and ye came unto me. Then shall the righteous answer him, saying, Lord, when saw we thee an hungred, and fed thee? or thirsty, and

gave thee *drink? When saw we thee a stranger, and took* thee *in? or naked, and clothed* thee*? Or when saw we thee sick, or in prison, and came unto thee? And the King shall answer and say unto them, Verily I say unto you, Inasmuch as ye have done* it *unto one of the least of these my brethren, ye have done* it *unto me. Then shall he say also unto them on the left hand, Depart from me, ye cursed, into everlasting fire, prepared for the devil and his angels: For I was an hungred, and ye gave me no meat: I was thirsty, and ye gave me no drink: I was a stranger, and ye took me not in: naked, and ye clothed me not: sick, and in prison, and ye visited me not. Then shall they also answer him, saying, Lord, when saw we thee an hungred, or athirst, or a stranger, or naked, or sick, or in prison, and did not minister unto thee? Then shall he answer them, saying, Verily I say unto you, Inasmuch as ye did* it *not to one of the least of these, ye did* it *not to me. And these shall go away into everlasting punishment: but the righteous into life eternal."*   (Matthew 25:31-46)

Chapter 5
Great White Throne Judgment

The previous four chapters have given us an up close and personal glimpse into the character of the judgments of God. We can identify with clarity the basis of the judgments and the individuals that will be associated with them. Yet, there is one last judgment that we must be aware of. It is grand in scale and monumental in impact as it stretches across time vastness of time, staking claims on souls from one end under the heavens to the other end. This judgment is known as 'The Great White Throne Judgment' and just as 'The Judgment Seat of Christ' will not be executed on the earth, nor will this great judgment take place on the earth. It will take place somewhere above the earth in the universe.

"And I saw a great white throne, and him that sat on it, from whose face the earth and the heaven fled away; and there was found no place for them." (Revelation 20:11)

But before moving into the sphere of 'The Great White Throne Judgment', let us view the events which immediately precede this specific judgment. We understand that the Judgment of the Nations takes place prior to the commencement of 'The Great White Throne Judgment'. However, there is a 1000-year Kingdom Age or Millennial Age that separates these two predetermined events. The Kingdom Age is an age of glory on earth, which cannot be overlooked in lieu of the pending judgment, as it is of immense importance in the scheme of all things. It is the glorious age and pinnacle of every preceding age that has come into existence since the foundation of the world. It is the glorious age because the Lord Jesus Christ will rule and reign in physical form on the earth. Yes, the Sovereign King will be seated on His Throne in Jerusalem and He will ensure that the will of the Father is done on Earth, even as it is done in Heaven. It will be an age of great peace that the world has never known. The nature of wild animals will be changed, and they will be as tamed pets so to speak.

"And righteousness shall be the girdle of his loins, and faithfulness the girdle of his reins. The wolf also shall dwell with the lamb, and the leopard shall lie down with the kid; and the calf and the young lion and the fatling together; and a little child shall lead them. And the cow and the bear shall feed; their young ones shall lie down together: and the lion shall eat straw like the ox. And the sucking child shall play on the hole of the asp, and the weaned child shall put his hand on the cockatrice' den." (Isaiah 11:5-8)

When Jesus is ruling on the throne, there will be no mistaking who the King of Kings and Lord of Lords is. Everyone will have knowledge of His sovereignty in the earth. Knowledge of the King will be global or universal because the conditions of this earthly realm will drastically change. He will exercise dominion over the spheres of culture to expand the Kingdom culture of God throughout the earth, even as far as the four corners of the world. Every area of society will be influenced by the culture of the Kingdom.

"They shall not hurt nor destroy in all my holy mountain: for the earth shall be full of the knowledge of the LORD, as the waters cover the sea." (Isaiah 11:9)

No one will be able to doubt or question the validity of the great Lord and King Jesus Christ because during this glorious age righteousness shall be the character of His rule. There will be no scandals as we see in this present age with world leaders across the globe. Judgment will be based on the divine laws and excellent will of God. There will be no interpreting or tweaking of the laws to suite man's shortcomings and failures. It will be absolute justice that is executed by the Lord Jesus Christ, so He will never be accused of unrighteous dealings with man during the Kingdom Age or Millennial Age.

"But with righteousness shall he judge the poor, and reprove with equity for the meek of the earth: and he shall smite the earth with the rod of his mouth, and with the breath of his lips shall he slay the wicked. And righteousness shall be the girdle of his loins, and faithfulness the girdle of his reins." (Isaiah 11:4-5)

Many environmental issues that prove to be hazardous to the health of humanity will be eradicated in this age. Air pollution that weakens the ozone layer will not exist. Chemical pollution and waste that has negatively impacted the water supply of the world will be removed and the waters will be cleansed. The damaging effects of pesticides and wide- spread diseases that have affected the land will be eliminated. And even weapons that cause mass destruction in the world will be done away with. In other words, everything that has promoted a short life span for humanity that we have seen in previous ages, will not be seen in the Kingdom Age. This will be a time of longevity for mankind, as many will live far beyond 100 years old. If someone happens to die at the age of 100, he will be considered to have died young or as a babe. The environmental changes that will have taken place will enrich the life expectancy of all those who will enter the Kingdom Age.

"There shall be no more thence and infant of days, nor an old man that hath not filled his days: for the child shall die an hundred years old; but the sinner being an hundred years old shall be accursed." (Isaiah 65:20)

The Kingdom Age will be a time of human elevation as they learn about the Lord and grasp understanding of His ways. The nations of the earth will come to Jerusalem every year to worship and pay homage to the Lord Jesus Christ. All the nations that come forth each year to worship will be blessed, but any nation that does not come to Jerusalem to worship will be punished by not having rain in their respective lands. For not coming to worship the King is a blatant form of disrespect.

"And it shall come to pass, that every one that is left of all the nations which came against Jerusalem shall even go up from year to year to worship the King, the LORD of hosts, and to keep the feast of tabernacles. And it shall be, that whoso will not come up of all the families of the earth unto Jerusalem to worship the King, the LORD of hosts, even upon them shall be no rain." (Zechariah 14:16-17)

The Kingdom Age is a time of immediacy concerning judgment because the Lord Jesus Christ will rule with an iron of rod. So, for the nations that are allowed to enter the

Kingdom Age, this means that sin of any form will be dealt with immediately and with the highest regard to the laws of the Kingdom. Many people will be surprised to know that things will operate much differently concerning sin or breaking laws than we see in this current age. This Age of Grace has spoiled humanity and has caused many to take advantage of the favor and mercy of the Lord. But this will not be the case in the Kingdom Age because Jesus will be functioning in a different role during the glorious Kingdom Age. Instead of being the sacrificial lamb who died for the sins of the world, He will be King and lion of the tribe of Judah. He will rule in sovereignty and righteousness, so the character of the Kingdom era will be that of His very own nature. It will be a righteous and holy era where there will be zero tolerance for sin.

"Thou shalt break them with a rod of iron; thou shalt dash them in pieces like a potter's vessel. Be wise now therefore, O ye kings: be instructed, ye judges of the earth. Serve the LORD with fear, and rejoice with trembling. Kiss the Son, lest he be angry, and ye perish from the way, when his wrath is kindled but a little. Blessed are all they that put their trust in him." (Psalms 2:9-12)

Once again, it will be a glorious and righteous age on earth. But when the 1000-year Kingdom Age comes to an end, Satan will be loosed from the bottomless pit, to try and deceive the nations. God will use Satan to expose the heart of the nations. Please understand that although the Kingdom Age is a glorious age, everyone living on earth at that time will not be submitted to God. When the Kingdom Age commences, the nations that are allowed entrance will not be born again believers. They will still have the old adamic or sin nature, and they will still give birth to children who will also have that sin nature. Sin will not be open and blatant as in the previous ages because Jesus will rule with a rod of iron, so people will not be so eager to boast in sin. Those who sin will be dealt immediate judgment according to God's statutes. Yet, even as righteous as the Kingdom Age will be, Satan will still be able to deceive some of the nations, and he will gather these nations to war against the Lord Jesus Christ. Satan will surround the city of Jerusalem in hopes of dethroning Jesus, but the Father God will send fire down from heaven to destroy this great army of nations that rose up against the King of Kings and Lord of Lords. Satan will then be casted into the lake of fire where he will be tormented forever.

"And when the thousand years are expired, Satan shall be loosed out of his prison, And shall go out to deceive the

nations which are in the four quarters of the earth, Gog and Magog, to gather them together to battle: the number of whom is as the sand of the sea. And they went up on the breadth of the earth, and compassed the camp of the saints about, and the beloved city: and fire came down from God out of heaven, and devoured them. And the devil that deceived them was cast into the lake of fire and brimstone, where the beast and the false prophet are, and shall be tormented day and night for ever and ever." (Revelation 20:7-10)

After Satan is cast into the lake of fire, there will be a resurrection of souls, but it will not be a resurrection of righteous souls. For this shall be the resurrection of the unrighteous, which includes all the people who rejected the salvation through Jesus Christ since time began. They were forbidden entrance into the Kingdom Age; therefore, they remained in the grave for the entire 1000 years of the Kingdom Age awaiting the time that they would be resurrected for judgment. This judgment is known as The Great White Throne Judgment. We know that it will not take place on earth just as the Judgment Seat of Christ does not take place on earth, but it takes place above the earth and somewhere in the universe. Just as believers who stood before the Judgments Seat of Christ to be judged on the basis of their good works and receive rewards of varying degrees, so it is with the unrighteous in this judgment. Those who stand before The Great White Throne Judgment will be judged according to their works, not on the basis of whether or not they are saved. The very fact that they are standing before this throne means that they are not saved. The underlying factor for the determination of their works and the degree of their punishment will be based on what is recorded in their book of life. Please understand that there is a difference between the book of life for an individual who lived on earth and the Book of Life that keeps a record of all who have eternal life in Christ.

"And I saw a great white throne, and him that sat on it, from whose face the earth and the heaven fled away; and there was found no place for them. And I saw the dead, small and great, stand before God; and the books were opened: and another book was opened, which is the book of life: and the dead were judged out of those things which were written in the books, according to their works. And the sea gave up the dead which were in it; and death and hell delivered up the dead which were in them: and they were judged every man according to their works." (Revelation 20:11-13)

Not only are these books different in what is housed within them, but before anyone in this judgment is sentenced, the Lord Jesus Christ will double-check to see if their names are included in the Book of Life because their fate is sealed for eternity. Even hell, which is a holding place for the wicked dead at this current time, will itself, be cast into the lake of fire, as there will no longer be a need for its existence. Justice will have finally been served regarding all of humanity.

"And death and hell were cast into the lake of fire. This is the second death. And whosoever was not found written in the book of life was cast into the lake of fire." (Revelation 20:14-15)

The final judgment of humanity is inevitable on all fronts and it marks a very pivotal moment in the full scope of God's eternal plan. As1 The White Throne Judgment is being carried out, God will be renovating the heaven and the earth, as the former will be no more. And when speaking of a new heaven and a new earth, it specifically refers to the earth and the heaven right above it, not the entire universe. This earth has been at the center of God's plan from the beginning because it served as the testing ground for humanity, God's most masterful creation. Yet, after the renovation of the earth, it shall be the dwelling place of both God and man. Nothing will every separate God from His creation again, as

He will now dwell with them and in them. It is a union that will never be interrupted or severed. It will be perpetual throughout all eternity. Amen.

Cynthia Alvarez

AUTHOR

Cynthia Alvarez is a dedicated servant of the Lord Jesus Christ. Her passion for the King and his Kingdom is undeniable as she continues to empower the Body of Christ in this hour. The goal of her work is to break believers out of the typical church pattern by acclimating them to the culture of the Kingdom of God. Being a published author and staunch supporter of the Kingdom of God, she has written several books to assist believers in understanding the Kingdom and its culture. Some of her most controversial books in this era are *Apostles, Prophets, and Revealed.* These books bring remarkable life altering revelation to readers in many essential ways, as we see believers across the globe in increased pursuit of the King and the Kingdom. The success of the Kingdom message through this work of literature has prompted Cynthia to continue writing books. *The Judgments of God* has become a masterpiece as it details the five judgments that God has appointed for humanity. It is crucial for all believers to secure their standing in the Lord and understand what awaits them in judgment. This book will open the eyes of believers and cause them to re-evaluate their individual standing in Christ. *The Judgments of God* is riveting and thought provoking on all front, as it has the ability of persuading every believer to make their calling and election sure in Christ and in the Kingdom of God.

A special thanks to all who have supported the endeavors of Cynthia Alvarez with your purchase of this book. May the blessings of our Lord Jesus Christ richly increase you above measure.

Cynthia Alvarez

The Judgments of God

Cynthia Alvarez

www.ingramcontent.com/pod-product-compliance
Lightning Source LLC
Chambersburg PA
CBHW052102110526
44591CB00013B/2320